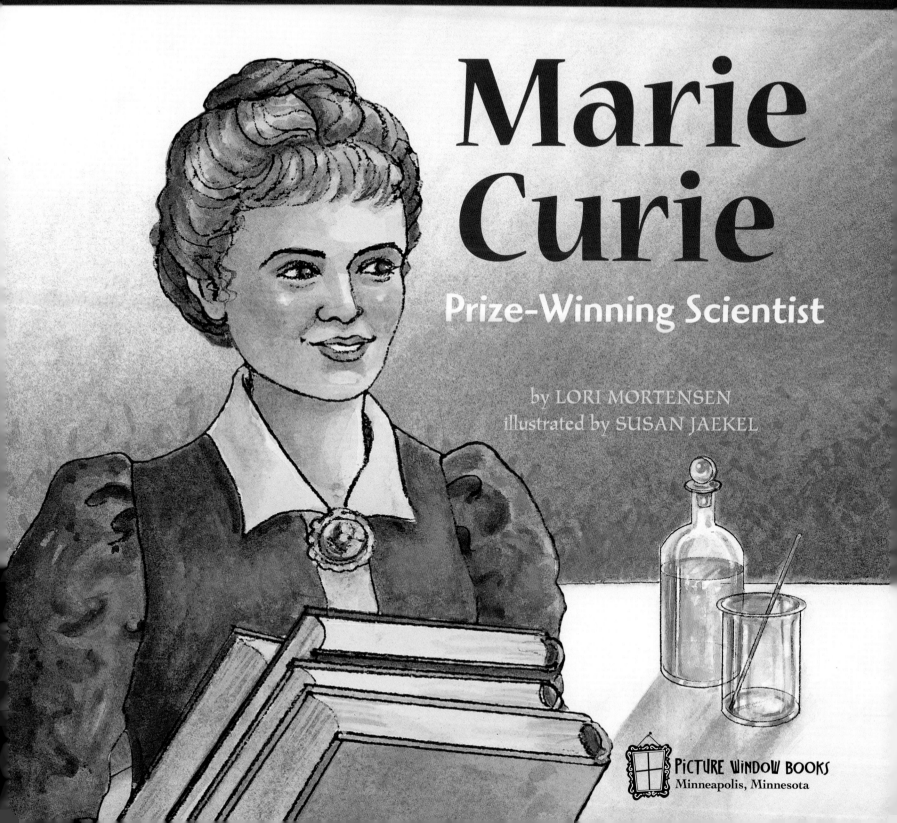

Marie Curie

Prize-Winning Scientist

by LORI MORTENSEN

illustrated by SUSAN JAEKEL

PICTURE WINDOW BOOKS
Minneapolis, Minnesota

Special thanks to our advisers for their expertise:

Andy Karam, Ph.D., CHP
Radiation Consultant and Adjunct Professor
Rochester Institute of Technology

Terry Flaherty, Ph.D.
Professor of English
Minnesota State University, Mankato

Editor: Shelly Lyons
Designers: Abbey Fitzgerald and Hilary Wacholz
Page Production: Michelle Biedscheid
Art Director: Nathan Gassman
Associate Managing Editor: Christianne Jones
The illustrations in this book were created with watercolor and pastel.
Photo Credit: Library of Congress, page 3

Picture Window Books
1710 Roe Crest Drive
North Mankato, MN 56003
www.capstonepub.com

Library of Congress Cataloging-in-Publication Data
Mortensen, Lori, 1955-
Marie Curie : prize-winning scientist / by Lori Mortensen ; illustrated by Susan Jaekel.
p. cm. — (Biographies)
Includes index.
ISBN-13: 978-1-4048-3731-7 (library binding)
1. Curie, Marie, 1867-1934—Juvenile literature. 2. Women chemists—Poland—
Biography—Juvenile literature. 3. Women chemists—France—Biography—Juvenile
literature. I. Jaekel, Susan M., ill. II. Title.
QD22.C8M68 2008
540.92—dc22   2007032885

Printed in the United States of America in Stevens Point, Wisconsin.
072013
007593R

Marie Curie was a great scientist. She discovered two elements that gave off invisible rays of energy. She called this sort of energy "radioactivity." Her research led to treatments for cancer and new ideas about energy.

Marie was the first woman to receive a Nobel Prize.

This is the story of
Marie Curie.

Marie was born in Poland on November 7, 1867. She was the youngest of five children. One day, one of her sisters was having trouble reading a schoolbook. Marie read it easily. Her parents were shocked.

Marie was only 4 years old.

Marie's family had many troubles. Her mother was sick with a lung disease. When Marie was 6, her father lost his job and their home.

Marie's family moved to a small apartment. It was noisy and crowded. But the noise did not stop Marie from studying. When she read, she could ignore everything else.

In 1883, Marie graduated from high school with top honors. She dreamed of becoming a scientist. But in Poland, girls were not allowed to go to college. And Marie's family did not have enough money to send her to a university in another country.

Reaching her dream seemed impossible.

Marie and her sister Bronya made a plan. They would study in France. Marie would work to pay for Bronya's schooling. Then, once Bronya graduated, she would work and pay for Marie's schooling.

Marie worked as a tutor and a nanny for
six years.

Finally, in 1891, Marie's dream came true. She enrolled at the Sorbonne, a major university in Paris. In three years, she earned advanced degrees in physics and mathematics.

She also met a scientist named Pierre Curie. Marie and Pierre married in 1895.

Marie studied a metal element called uranium. She wanted to study uranium because scientists knew it gave off invisible rays of energy. She wondered where the rays came from.

Marie began testing rocks to find out if other elements gave off rays, too. Marie decided two elements found in the rocks were radioactive. Those two elements were thorium as well as uranium. She called the energy "radioactivity."

Marie's experiments were so exciting that she and Pierre soon began working together.

One day, Marie began testing a black rock. The rock was more radioactive than thorium or uranium. Marie discovered a new element in the rock. She named the element "polonium," after Poland. Polonium was 400 times more radioactive than uranium.

After Marie removed the polonium, the rock was still radioactive. She knew another radioactive element was inside the rock. Marie called that element "radium."

The amount of radium in the rock was so small that it was invisible. Marie ground up rocks for four years to gather more radium. By 1902, she had gathered a tiny sample. It weighed less than a feather.

The radium glowed with a soft blue light. It was 900 times more radioactive than uranium.

In 1903, Marie and Pierre received the Nobel Prize in Physics. Marie was the first woman to receive a Nobel Prize. Some people thought she should not receive the award, because she was a woman.

In 1911, Marie accepted a second Nobel Prize, the Nobel Prize in Chemistry. She was the first person to receive two Nobel Prizes.

Marie dedicated her life to the study of radiation. Yet the work she felt so strongly about also made her sick. At the time, nobody knew about the harmful effects of radiation. On July 4, 1934, Marie Curie died of a blood disease that may have been caused by radiation. She was 67.

Marie's discoveries helped save millions of lives and changed the scientific world. Radiation has been used to treat cancer. Her ideas about the atom helped lead to the discovery of nuclear energy.

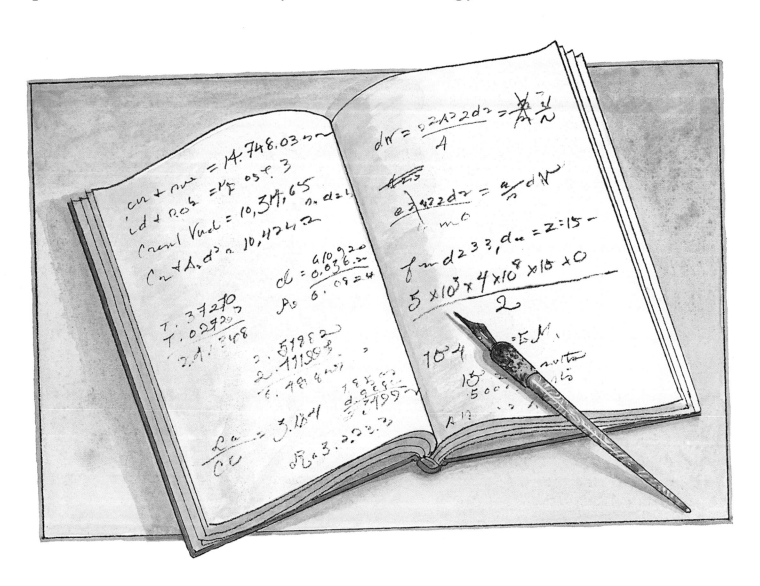

The Life of Marie Curie

1867	Born in Warsaw, Poland, on November 7
1883	Graduated from high school
1891	Enrolled in the Sorbonne in Paris, France
1893	Earned a degree in physics
1894	Earned a degree in mathematics
1895	Married Pierre Curie
1898	Discovered polonium and radium with Pierre
1902	Produced a sample of radium
1903	Received the Nobel Prize in Physics
1906	Pierre accidentally killed by a horse-drawn wagon; Marie becomes the first female professor at the Sorbonne
1911	Received the Nobel Prize in Chemistry
1914–1918	Assembled X-ray machines to help soldiers injured in World War I
1934	Died on July 4

Did You Know?

~ Marie was born Marya Sklodowska. Her family called her "Manya." She changed her name to Marie when she moved to France. She had one brother and three sisters.

~ Marie and Pierre had two daughters. Irene grew up to be a great scientist, too. In 1935, she and her husband, Frederic Joliot, earned a Nobel Prize in Chemistry.

~ During World War I (1914–1918), Marie put together mobile X-ray machines to help doctors identify the broken bones of injured soldiers. She and her daughter Irene took patients' X-rays themselves.

~ Marie was the first person to earn two Nobel Prizes and the only person who has received Nobel Prizes in different areas of science—physics and chemistry. She was also the first woman to earn a doctorate degree in Europe. And she was the first female professor at a French university, the Sorbonne.

~ Marie did not patent, or get the rights to, her discoveries. She believed it was more important to share her scientific information than to make money.

~ Marie was exposed to high levels of radiation. Today her notebooks are still radioactive. They still must be handled with care.

Glossary

atom — the smallest unit of an element

element — a substance made of atoms that cannot be broken down into simpler substances

Nobel Prize — any of six awards given each year by the Nobel Foundation

nuclear energy — the energy stored in an atom; it is used to power homes, submarines, and spacecraft

polonium — a silvery-gray element that is very radioactive

radioactivity — the process of giving off rays

radium — a silvery-white element that is radioactive and is found in uranium

thorium — a silver-colored element that is weakly radioactive

uranium — a silver-colored element that is weakly radioactive

To Learn More

More Books to Read

McCormick, Lisa Wade. *Marie Curie*. New York: Children's Press, 2006.

Meachen Rau, Dana. *Marie Curie*. Minneapolis: Compass Point Books, 2001.

Steele, Philip. *Marie Curie: The Woman Who Changed the Course of Science*. Washington, D.C.: National Geographic, 2006.

Waxman, Laura Hamilton. *Marie Curie*. Minneapolis: Lerner Publications, 2004.

On the Web

FactHound offers a safe, fun way to find Web sites related to topics in this book. All of the sites on FactHound have been researched by our staff.

1. Visit *www.facthound.com*

2. Type in this special code: 1404837310

3. Click on the FETCH IT button.

Your trusty FactHound will fetch the best sites for you!

Index

Look for all of the books in the Biographies series:

Abraham Lincoln: *Lawyer, President, Emancipator*

Albert Einstein: *Scientist and Genius*

Amelia Earhart: *Female Pioneer in Flight*

Benjamin Franklin: *Writer, Inventor, Statesman*

Booker T. Washington: *Teacher, Speaker, and Leader*

Cesar Chavez: *Champion and Voice of Farmworkers*

Frederick Douglass: *Writer, Speaker, and Opponent of Slavery*

George Washington: *Farmer, Soldier, President*

George Washington Carver: *Teacher, Scientist, and Inventor*

Harriet Tubman: *Hero of the Underground Railroad*

Jackie Robinson: *Hero and Athlete*

Marie Curie: *Prize-Winning Scientist*

Martha Washington: *First Lady of the United States*

Martin Luther King Jr.: *Preacher, Freedom Fighter, Peacemaker*

Pocahontas: *Peacemaker and Friend to the Colonists*

Sally Ride: *Astronaut, Scientist, Teacher*

Sojourner Truth: *Preacher for Freedom and Equality*

Susan B. Anthony: *Fighter for Freedom and Equality*

Thomas Edison: *Inventor, Scientist, and Genius*

Thomas Jefferson: *A Founding Father of the United States of America*